LOVE IS...
MANDALA
COLORING BOOK

CRYSTAL
COLORING BOOKS

ISBN-13: 978-1986171465
ISBN-10: 1986171469

Love is...

looking forward
together
not back

Love is...
the best
medicine

Love is...
being
together through
things that should
tear you apart-

Love is...
being there when
they need a hug

Love is ...

when
you just need to
hold each other

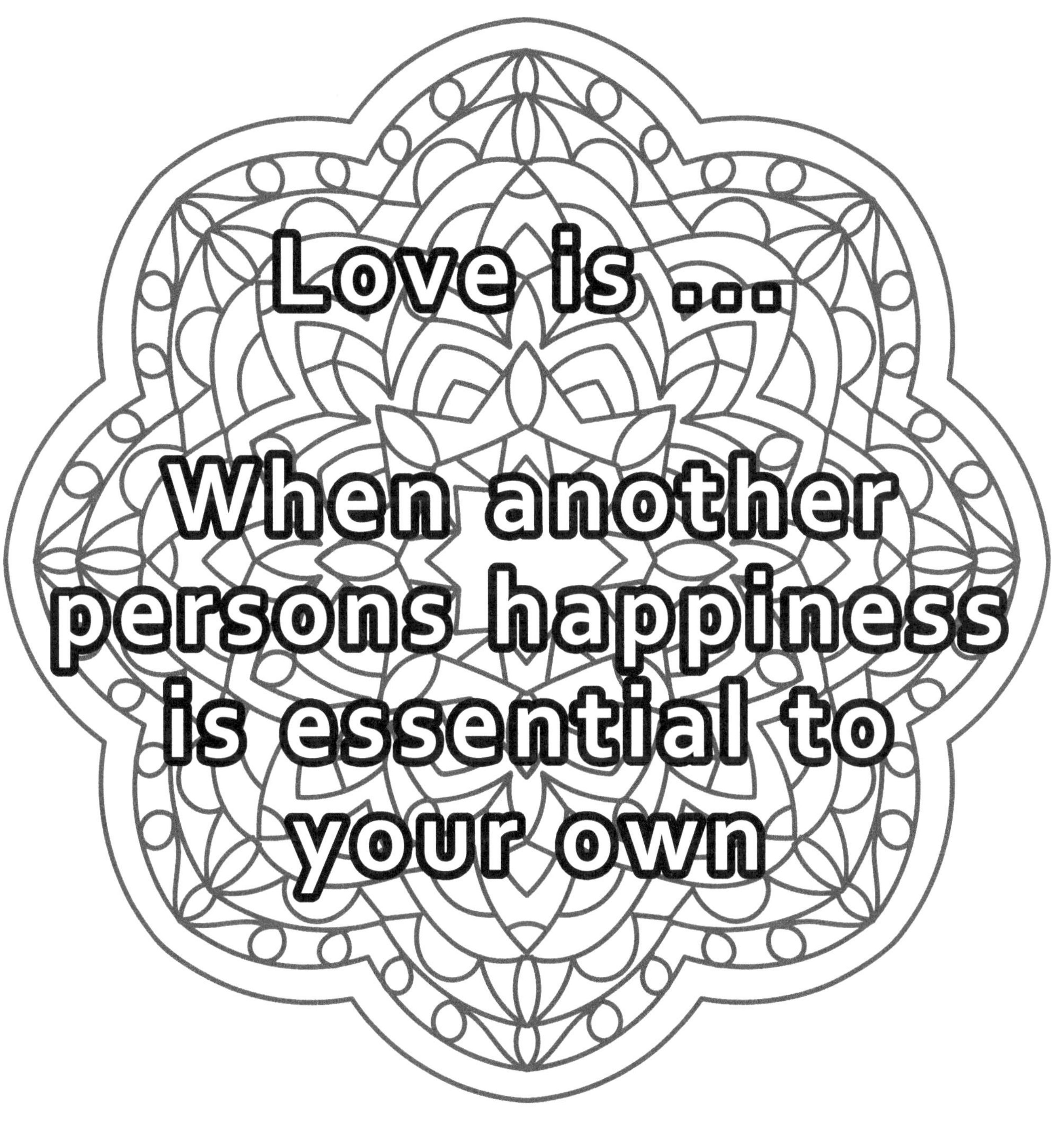

Love is ...

When another persons happiness is essential to your own

Love is ...
what the heart feels

Love is ...
the best thing that
will ever
happen to
you

Love is ...

more than just
good sex

Love is ...
honesty and trust

Love is ...
reaching your
dreams
together

Love is ...

spending your life
making each
other
happy

Love is ...
sailing rough seas
together

Love is ...
a kiss

Love is ...

just a word until
you meet some-
one who gives it
meaning

Love is ...
never wanting to
be apart

Love is ...

wishing they were
beside you when
you fall asleep

Love is ...

like a warm
breeze you can
feel it but you
can't see it

Love is ...

risking everything
to be
together

Love is ...
missing someone

COLOR TEST PAGE

9 781986 171465